KiDS CAN COOK!

DISGUSTING EATS

NASTY, BUT TASTY RECIPES

BY MARNE VENTURA

CAPSTONE PRESS
a capstone imprint

Edge Books are published by Capstone Press,
1710 Roe Crest Drive, North Mankato, Minnesota 56003
www.mycapstone.com

Library of Congress Cataloging-in-Publication Data
Names: Ventura, Marne, author.
Title: Disgusting eats : nasty, but tasty recipes / by Marne Ventura.
Description: Mankato, Minnesota : Capstone Press, [2017] | Series: Edge Books.
    Kids can cook! | Audience: Ages 10–13. | Audience: Grades 4-6. |
    Includes bibliographical references.
Identifiers: LCCN 2016028370 (print) | LCCN 2016031734 (ebook) |
    ISBN 9781515738121 (library binding) | ISBN 9781515738244 (eBook PDF)
Subjects: LCSH: Cooking--Juvenile literature. | Food craft--Juvenile literature. |
    LCGFT: Cookbooks.
Classification: LCC TX652.5 .V46 2017 (print) | LCC TX652.5 (ebook) | DDC 641.5123--dc23
LC record available at https://lccn.loc.gov/2016028370

Summary
Easy-to-follow instructions and cooking tips teach young readers how to cook a variety
of gross-looking, yet delicious recipes.

Editorial Credits
Aaron Sautter, editor; Sarah Bennett, designer; Laura Manthe, production specialist

Photo Credits
All photographs by Capstone Studio/Karon Dubke, Sarah Schuette, Food Stylist

Printed in Canada.
010021S17

TABLE OF CONTENTS

Looks Gross – Tastes Great! 4

The Gross Gourmet 6

SICKENING SNACKS

Snails a La Slime 8

Severed Finger Sandwiches 10

Booger Dip 12

REVOLTING SIDE DISHES

Cheesy Meat Head 14

Bloody Bone Soup 16

Road Kill Salad 18

NAUSEATING MAIN MEALS

Slimy Pesto Baby Rat Nest 20

Maggoty Chili 24

DISGUSTING DESSERTS

Worms in Dirt 26

Bloodshot Eyeball Cupcakes 28

Bloody Bandages 30

Read More 32

Internet Sites 32

LOOKS GROSS –
TASTES GREAT!

Has anyone has ever told you not to play with your food? Well here's your chance to ignore that! Get ready to gross out your family and friends with these disgustingly easy recipes.

Whether you want to eat squiggly worms, maggot–filled chili, or booger dip, you'll have tons of fun learning to make these sickening snacks and meals. Plus, you can surprise your friends when they realize that these dishes look revolting, but taste great!

SAFETY FIRST

Cooking well requires a lot of care, which includes being careful around tools and equipment. Follow these simple rules to stay safe in the kitchen.

- Always ask an adult for permission to use sharp knives, hot stoves, and electric appliances. When in doubt, ask an adult to help you use them.

- Always cut your food on a cutting board. Avoid cutting your fingers by holding food with your fingertips curved inward. You should also always make sure that the knife blade points away from your body as you're cutting.

- Tie back long hair and tuck in loose clothing to avoid catching them on fire.

- Avoid spreading germs by always washing your hands with soap and warm water. Do this both before and after preparing food.

- Use dry oven mitts or pot holders to handle hot dishes, pots, and pans.

- Always wash fruits and vegetables before preparing them.

COOKING TIPS AND TRICKS

The best cooks usually have a plan in place before beginning any meal. Follow these tips in the kitchen to cook like a pro.

- Read all the way through a recipe before you begin. Then gather together the equipment and ingredients you'll need to make the recipe.

- Clear your workspace of clutter and keep the surface clean.

- Keep things simple by putting food and ingredients away as you work.

- Stay in the kitchen while you cook to avoid food disasters.

- Clean up completely when you're done.

TEMPERATURE

Fahrenheit	Celsius
325°	160°
350°	180°
375°	190°
400°	200°
425°	220°
450°	230°

PROPERLY MEASURING INGREDIENTS

- If possible, use transparent glass or plastic cups so you can check measurements at eye level.

- Measuring cups with a handle and spout are useful for liquid ingredients.

- Spoon dry ingredients into a measuring cup and level it with a knife.

- Measuring spoons are good for both liquid and dry ingredients.

MEASUREMENTS

1/8 teaspoon	0.6 gram or milliliter
1/4 teaspoon	1.25 g or ml
1/2 teaspoon	2.5 g or ml
1 teaspoon	5 g or ml
1 tablespoon	15 g or ml
1/4 cup	57 g (dry) or 60 ml (liquid)
1/3 cup	75 g (dry) or 80 ml (liquid)
1/2 cup	114 g (dry) or 125 ml (liquid)
3/4 cup	170 g (dry) or 175 ml (liquid)
1 cup	227 g (dry) or 240 ml (liquid)
1 quart	950 ml
1 ounce	28 g
1 pound	454 g

THE GROSS GOURMET

Want to learn some tricks for creating your own gross eats? It's easy! Look around for something disgusting. Say you want to make some edible used cotton swabs. You just need to find some great-tasting foods to represent this gross household item. A pretzel stick coated with white chocolate works great. Just stick a mini-marshmallow on each end of the pretzel stick to represent the cotton tip. Then dip each end in caramel sauce, and you've got a delicious earwax-covered treat!

Here are some other foods with yucky qualities to give you some ideas and get you started:

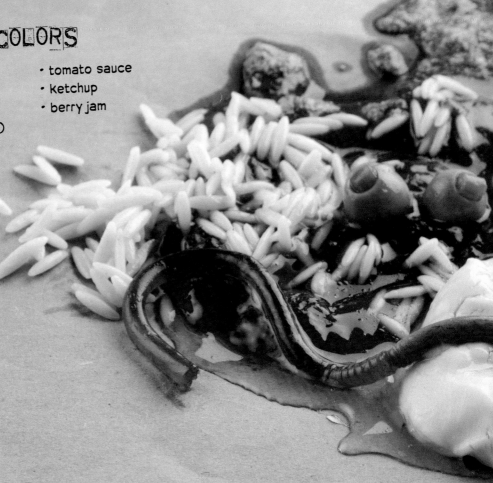

SLIME IN MANY COLORS

- mayonnaise
- creamy Alfredo sauce
- vanilla pudding
- green salsa (salsa verde)
- fruit gelatins
- caramel sauce
- peanut butter
- honey
- tomato juice
- tomato sauce
- ketchup
- berry jam

PEELED SKIN OR ROAD KILL

(add slimy sauce for extra grossness)

- boiled bacon
- pepperoni
- salami
- chopped beef
- sausage
- chopped chicken

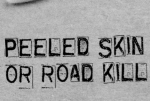

INSECTS, WORMS, AND RODENT PARTS

- raisins
- dates
- craisins
- crispy chow mein noodles
- shredded wheat cereal
- coconut
- boiled spaghetti
- grated zucchini
- boiled macaroni
- boiled egg noodles

ALL IN THE PRESENTATION

Serving up disgusting foods in creative ways is a great way to turn up the gross-out factor. For example, fill a glass jar with peeled grapes or pickled pearl onions. Then put on a label that says "PICKLED EYEBALLS." Or put out a plate of bacon bits sprinkled over some ketchup smeared on the plate. Then add a sign that says "FRESHLY PEELED SCABS."

Use your imagination to find ways to really gross people out!

SLIMY EYEBALLS

- pearl onions
- peeled grapes
- boiled eggs

freshly peeled scabs . . . yum!

SNAILS A LA SLIME

MAKES 24 SNAILS

Need a quick and easy finger food for your next scary movie night? Look no further. This recipe puts a fun twist on pigs in a blanket — it's Snails á la Slime! Refrigerated dough makes this recipe quick and easy while slimy condiments make it gross and yucky.

INGREDIENTS

1 can (8 ounces) of refrigerated
  crescent roll dough
24 mini smoked sausages
  (14 to 16 ounces)
crispy chow mein noodles
pickle relish
ketchup
mustard

EQUIPMENT

baking sheet
cooking spray
sharp cooking knife
cutting board

Try This!

For slimy cheese snails, cut some string cheese sticks in half to use instead of the small sausages. Serve the snails with pesto slime (see page 22) or bloody spaghetti sauce.

STEPS

1 Preheat oven to 375° F. Spray the baking sheet with cooking spray.

2 Separate the dough into eight triangles. Cut each triangle lengthwise to make three smaller triangles. Now you have 24 triangles, one for each sausage.

3 Place a sausage at the wide end of a triangle of dough. Roll the dough around the sausage. Leave about 1 inch (2.5 centimeters) of the pointed end extended.

4 Fold the pointed end back on itself to make the snail's head. Then insert two chow mein noodles for antennae.

5 Bake for 15 minutes or until golden brown.

6 Serve the snails on a plate with a slimy trail of pickle relish, ketchup, or mustard. Put extra slime on the backs of the snails for added grossness.

SEVERED FINGER SANDWICHES

MAKES 12 SANDWICHES

Don't bite off more than you can chew. Uh, oh — looks like someone already did! These digits are oozing with tuna slime. Even the bloody fingernails look nasty.

INGREDIENTS

1 can (11 ounces) of refrigerated
   breadstick dough
1 small yellow onion
1 stalk celery
2 cans (7 ounces) of
   water-packed tuna
1/4 cup mayonnaise
1/8 teaspoon salt
1/8 teaspoon pepper
12 almond slices
tomato sauce

EQUIPMENT

baking sheet
sharp cooking knife
oven mitt or pot holders
wire rack
cutting board
medium mixing bowl
mixing spoon

STEPS

1. Preheat the oven to 375° F.

2. Separate bread sticks and place on ungreased baking sheet.

3. Cut slits in the top of the bread sticks to imitate knuckles.

4. Bake the breadsticks for 13 to 15 minutes or until golden brown.

5. Remove breadsticks from oven and cool on wire rack.

6. Wash, peel, and finely chop the onion and celery.

7. Open and drain the cans of tuna.

8. In the bowl mix together the tuna, chopped onion and celery, mayonnaise, salt, and pepper.

9. Slice breadsticks lengthwise.

10. Spread the tuna salad inside the sliced breadsticks.

11. Cut a small slit in the end of each breadstick. Then insert a sliced almond for each fingernail.

12. Add a little tomato sauce to both ends of the breadstick "fingers" to make them look bloody.

DID YOU KNOW?

Afternoon teatime was popular in the 1800s in England. Dainty sandwiches were served as a snack. They were often called finger sandwiches because they were small enough to hold and eat with two fingers.

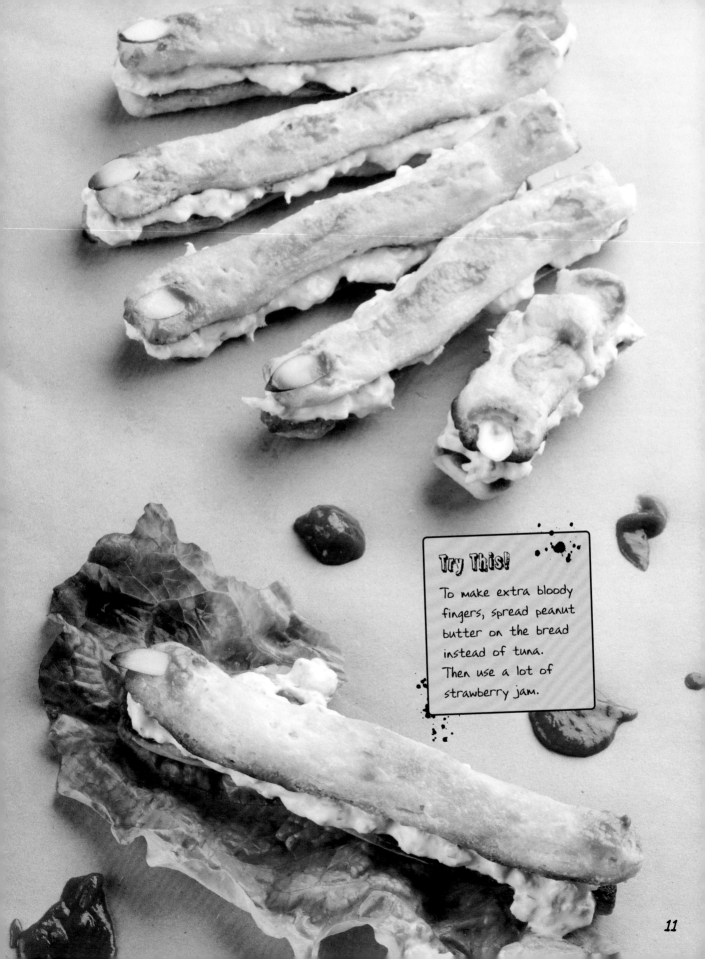

11

BOOGER DIP

MAKES 8 SERVINGS

Need a quick way to make food look repulsive? Just add some boogers! With slimy green avocado, bits of blood-red tomato, and chunks of red onion, this booger dip is seriously disgusting — and delicious!

INGREDIENTS

2 ripe avocados
2 Roma tomatoes
1 small red onion
1 teaspoon lemon juice
$1/4$ teaspoon salt
$1/4$ teaspoon pepper
$1/4$ teaspoon garlic powder
$1/4$ teaspoon onion powder
$1/2$ teaspoon chili powder

EQUIPMENT

sharp cooking knife
cutting board
mixing spoon
medium mixing bowl
fork

STEPS

1. Cut each avocado in half. Remove the pit. Use a spoon to scoop the avocado from the skin into the bowl.

2. Mash the avocado with a fork until smooth.

3. Wash the tomatoes and cut out the stems. Chop finely and add to the avocado.

4. Mince about $1/4$ cup of red onion and add to the avocado.

5. Add lemon juice, salt, pepper, garlic powder, onion powder, and chili powder. Stir all the ingredients until blended together well.

Serving Ideas

* Scoop up the boogers with blue corn tortilla chips.
* Add a dollop of booger dip to chili, tacos, or burritos.
* Smear some booger dip on your favorite sandwiches.
* Add some dip to a hamburger for, you guessed it — a booger burger!

DID YOU KNOW?
Ninety percent of the avocados eaten in the United States are grown in central and southern California.

CHEESY MEAT HEAD

MAKES 8 SERVINGS

The next time you invite your friends over for a party, ask them if they'd like a snack. Then surprise them and gross them out with this vile skinned-head cheeseball! After they stop retching, they'll be amazed that you made such a great tasting treat.

INGREDIENTS

1 package (8 ounces) cream cheese
1/2 cup crumbled blue cheese
1/2 cup shredded cheddar cheese
2 tablespoons minced onion
1/2 tablespoon Worcestershire sauce
2 green olives with pimentos
shelled pistachio nuts
1/2 pound thinly sliced deli ham
1 box snack crackers

EQUIPMENT

large mixing bowl
plastic wrap
serving platter
sharp cooking knife
cutting board

Try This!

If you don't like ham, try using other deli meats like salami or prosciutto instead. Or smear the head with ketchup to make it look bloody and gross.

STEPS

1. In a large bowl, mix the cream cheese, blue cheese, cheddar cheese, onion, and Worcestershire sauce until well blended.

2. Cover the cheese ball with plastic wrap and chill in refrigerator for at least 1 hour.

3. Take out the cheese ball and place on a serving platter. Form the ball into a skull shape with your hands.

4. Press the olives into the eye sockets.

5. Press the pistachios into the mouth opening for teeth.

6. Cut the ham into small pieces. Cover the cheese skull with ham.

7. Serve with crackers.

BLOODY BONE SOUP

MAKES 4 SERVINGS

Arr! A pirate's life is a hard one. How do pirates get through a busy day of raiding ships at sea? They fill up with the ultimate comfort food — blood and bones! This quick soup makes for a hearty lunch or dinner. Shiver me timbers, it's good!

SKULL AND CROSSBONE CROUTONS

INGREDIENTS

4 slices of bread
¼ cup olive oil
garlic powder
dried basil

EQUIPMENT

kitchen scissors
small bottle cap
cutting board
baking sheet
oven mitt or pot holders
pastry brush

STEPS

1. Preheat the oven to 325° F.

2. Use kitchen scissors to cut two bones and a skull from each slice of bread. Cut a triangle for the nose. Punch out eyeholes using a small bottle cap.

3. Place the skulls and bones on a baking sheet and bake for 8 minutes.

4. Remove from the oven and turn the bread pieces over.

5. Return to the oven and bake for 8 more minutes.

6. Remove from the oven.

7. Brush olive oil on both sides of the bread pieces.

8. Sprinkle each side with garlic powder and basil.

9. Return to the oven and bake for 3 to 5 more minutes, until golden and crispy.

BLOOD SOUP

INGREDIENTS

1 (14 ounce) can diced tomatoes
1 cup roasted red peppers, drained
1 cup cream
2 teaspoons salt
¼ teaspoon black pepper
¼ cup grated Parmesan cheese

EQUIPMENT

blender
large saucepan
wooden spoon

STEPS

1. Place tomatoes and red peppers in a blender. Cover tightly and blend on high until smooth.

2. Pour the tomato mixture into a large saucepan. Bring to a boil over medium heat, stirring occasionally.

3. Reduce the heat to low. Add the cream, salt, and pepper.

4. Heat until warm, but do not boil.

5. To serve, float a skull and two bone croutons on top of each bowl of soup. Sprinkle with one or two tablespoons of Parmesan cheese. Drizzle a spoonful of soup over the skull and crossbones for an extra bloody look.

ROAD KILL SALAD

MAKES 4 SALADS

Ever see a dead animal on the road? Don't waste it. Make a tasty salad with it! At least, that's what you can tell your friends. The walnut halves look like little brains and the cut strawberries resemble bloody hearts. Be sure to top it off with some cockroach dates and blood-clot dressing.

INGREDIENTS

⅛ tablespoon butter
2 tablespoons sugar
½ cup unbroken walnut halves
1 stick of celery
8 pitted dates
8 medium sized strawberries
1 head of lettuce
2 tablespoons raspberry or
   strawberry jam
1 tablespoon rice vinegar
⅓ cup olive oil
⅛ teaspoon salt
⅛ teaspoon black pepper
¼ cup crumbled blue cheese
   (optional)

EQUIPMENT

medium skillet
wooden spoon
plates
sharp cooking knife
cutting board
jar with a lid

Try This!

Candied walnuts in a
clear glass jar look just
like little brains in a
mad scientist's laboratory.
Try labeling the jar as
"Squirrel Brains" and hand
some out the next time
your friends come over.

STEPS

1 In a medium skillet, stir the butter, sugar, and
   walnuts over medium high heat. Continue to stir
   gently for about five minutes until the nuts are
   covered with a golden brown candy coating.

2 Transfer the nuts to a plate to cool. Separate
   them so they don't stick together.

3 Cut thin slivers from the celery to look like
   insect antennae. Stick two in the end of each
   date to look like cockroach antennae.

4 Wash and dry the strawberries and remove the
   stems. Slice each strawberry in half, top to
   bottom, to make heart shapes.

5 Wash and dry the lettuce. Tear or cut into
   bite-size pieces. Divide evenly between
   four plates.

6 Top the plates of lettuce with four walnut
   "brains," two "cockroach" dates, and four
   strawberry "hearts." If you wish, sprinkle on a
   tablespoon of crumbled blue cheese "mold."

7 To make "blood-clot" dressing, place the jam,
   vinegar, olive oil, salt, and pepper in the jar.
   Put the lid tightly on the jar and shake well.

8 Serve the salads with the "blood-clot"
   dressing drizzled over the top.

SLIMY PESTO BABY RAT NEST

MAKES 6 SERVINGS

This is no ordinary plate of pasta! First tell your family that you're going to serve them a delicious spaghetti dinner. Then watch their looks of surprise and horror when they see disgusting little rats staring at them from their dinner plates!

RATBALLS

INGREDIENTS

1 to 2 small carrots
1 pound lean ground beef
$\frac{1}{2}$ cup dry bread crumbs
1 egg, beaten
3 tablespoons milk
$\frac{1}{2}$ teaspoon salt
$\frac{1}{4}$ teaspoon pepper
$\frac{1}{2}$ teaspoon onion powder
chow mein noodles

EQUIPMENT

baking sheet
aluminum foil
wire rack
carrot peeler
sharp cooking knife
cutting board
mixing bowl

STEPS

1. Preheat the oven to 375° F.

2. Line a baking sheet with foil. Place a wire rack on the baking sheet.

3. Wash and peel the carrots. Make 48 thin slices.

4. In a large bowl, mix the ground beef, bread crumbs, egg, milk, salt, pepper, and onion powder.

5. Divide the meat mixture evenly into 24 balls. Each ball should be a little larger than a golf ball. Then form the balls into teardrop-shaped baby rats.

6. Place the baby rats on the wire rack and bake in the oven for 30 minutes.

7. Remove the baby rats from the oven. Allow to cool for 5 to 10 minutes.

8. For each baby rat, add carrots for ears. Use small pieces of chow mein noodles to make eyes. Use large chow mein noodles for tails. You can also use chow mein noodles to make whiskers if you wish.

SLIMY PESTO

INGREDIENTS

2 cups fresh basil leaves
  (packed tightly)
3/4 cup grated Parmesan cheese
3/4 cup olive oil
3 cloves garlic, peels removed
1/4 cup pine nuts

EQUIPMENT

food processor or blender

STEPS

1 Add all of the ingredients
  to the blender or
  food processor.

2 Cover and blend on medium
  speed for 2 to 3 minutes or
  until smooth.

> **Try This!**
>
> Try making a bloody
> rat's nest by using a
> jar of red spaghetti
> sauce instead of pesto.

RAT'S NEST

INGREDIENTS

4 quarts water
1 teaspoon salt
1 pound spaghetti noodles
1 can black beans, drained
  (optional)

EQUIPMENT

large saucepan
wooden spoon
colander

STEPS

1 Add water and salt to a large saucepan.
  Bring to a boil.

2 Add the spaghetti noodles, a handful
  at a time, to the boiling water.
  Stir with a wooden spoon to separate.

3 Boil 9 to 13 minutes, or until tender,
  stirring occasionally.

4 Drain in a colander, and then return the
  pasta to the large saucepan.

5 Pour the pesto sauce over the noodles
  and stir to coat the pasta.

6 To serve, divide the pasta evenly between
  six plates and then arrange four meaty
  rats on top of each nest. If desired,
  sprinkle on some black beans to simulate
  disgusting rat droppings!

MAGGOTY CHILI

MAKES 4-6 SERVINGS

Imagine chewy, slimy maggots floating on a bowl of bloody meat. It's enough to gag a fly! But this hearty beef and bean dish, topped with tiny pasta, is actually really tasty. Plus, every cook worth his salt needs a good, gross chili recipe!

CHILI

INGREDIENTS

1 medium onion
2 cloves garlic
2 teaspoons oil
1 pound lean ground beef
1 tablespoon chili powder
1/4 teaspoon salt
1/4 teaspoon black pepper
1 can (14 ounces) diced tomatoes
1 can (6 ounces) tomato paste
3/4 cup of water
1 can pinto beans

EQUIPMENT

sharp cooking knife
cutting board
large saucepan
wooden spoon

STEPS

1. Peel and chop the onion.

2. Peel and mince the garlic.

3. Heat the oil over medium heat in a large saucepan.

4. Add the onion and garlic to the saucepan. Cook and stir with a wooden spoon for about 2 minutes, or until the onion looks soft.

5. Add the ground beef to the pan. Break it up with the wooden spoon. Stir and cook until the beef is no longer pink.

6. Add the chili powder, salt, pepper, diced tomatoes, tomato paste, and water. Stir to blend and bring to a boil. Then cover and reduce heat to low. Simmer for 15 minutes.

7. Open and drain the beans. Add to the pan. Cover the pan and continue to simmer the chili for another 15 minutes.

DID YOU KNOW?

Orzo is just one of hundreds of different pasta shapes. Pasta is often made into long strings, such as spaghetti or linguini. But it can also be made into shells, ribbons, bow ties, letters, or wagon wheels!

Try This!

Pump up the gross factor by adding some acini di pepe pasta to the orzo. These tiny pasta pieces look just like little maggot eggs!

MAGGOTS

INGREDIENTS

2 cups water
½ teaspoon salt
¼ cup orzo pasta

EQUIPMENT

medium saucepan
colander

STEPS

1. Bring the water and salt to a boil over medium heat.

2. Add the orzo pasta and boil for 9 minutes.

3. Drain the pasta in a colander.

4. To serve, fill bowls with chili and top each with about 3 tablespoons of the orzo pasta maggots.

WORMS IN DIRT

MAKES 16 BROWNIES, 100 WORMS

What's grosser than a bunch of slimy earthworms in the mud? Eating them! Try making up a plate of these to serve for dessert. At first your friends will be grossed out. But when they take a bite, they'll agree — worms in dirt are delish!

DID YOU KNOW?
Brownies are an American invention from the late 1800s. They are considered both a cookie and a cake.

INGREDIENTS

3 cups water
6 ounce box of raspberry gelatin mix
3 packets (¼ ounce each) of unflavored
    gelatin mix
¾ cup whipping cream
one box of brownie mix
oil (check directions on brownie mix)
eggs (check directions on brownie mix)
chocolate syrup

EQUIPMENT

1 quart waxed cardboard milk carton
scissors
100 flexible straws
medium saucepan
wooden spoon
mixing bowl
8- x 8-inch (20- x 20-cm) pan
oven mitt or pot holder
rolling pin

STEPS

1 Pull on each straw to stretch out the flexed part.

2 Open the top of the milk carton and cut off the top creased section. Wash the carton with warm soapy water and rinse well. Then fill with enough straws to fit tightly inside the carton.

3 Bring 3 cups of water to a full boil in the saucepan. Remove from heat.

4 Add the raspberry and unflavored gelatin mix. Stir with a wooden spoon until completely dissolved.

5 Allow the liquid to cool until it's no longer steaming. Then stir in the whipping cream.

6 Pour the gelatin mixture into the carton to fill up the straws.

7 Place the carton in the refrigerator and allow gelatin to chill overnight.

8 Prepare the brownie mix according to the package directions. Cool completely.

9 Take the carton out of the refrigerator and remove the straws. To get the worms out, place the straws on a clean surface. Gently roll the rolling pin along the length of each straw. The worm will come out the other end.

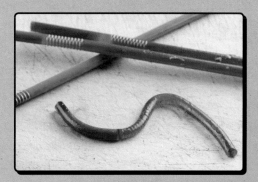

10 To serve, crumble brownies onto a plate or bowl and top with a few worms. Drizzle some chocolate syrup over the top to create a squirming, muddy pile of tasty worms!

Try This!

Crush some chocolate wafer cookies into crumbs. Place a few worms and some cookie crumbs in the bottom of transparent cups. Prepare some instant chocolate pudding and pour on top of the worms in each cup. Top with more crumbs and worms.

BLOODSHOT EYEBALL CUPCAKES

MAKES 12 CUPCAKES

Do you dare to eat something that's staring back at you? These gross bloodshot eyeball cupcakes are easy to make and taste great. Learn the trick of squirting frosting from a plastic bag, and you'll be creating all kinds of disgusting decorations.

CUPCAKES

INGREDIENTS

1 cup all-purpose flour
3/4 cup sugar
3/4 teaspoon baking soda
1/4 teaspoon salt
1/4 teaspoon baking powder
1/2 cup water
1/3 cup unsweetened cocoa powder
1/2 cup butter, softened
1 egg
1 teaspoon vanilla

EQUIPMENT

muffin tin
paper baking cups
medium mixing bowl
medium saucepan
small mixing bowl
oven mitt or pot holder
wooden spoon
toothpick
wire rack

STEPS

1 Preheat the oven to 350° F.

2 Place paper baking cups in a muffin tin.

3 In a medium bowl, mix the flour, sugar, baking soda, salt, and baking powder.

4 Add the water, cocoa powder, and butter to the saucepan.

5 Stir over medium heat until the cocoa is dissolved and the butter is melted. Remove from the heat and allow to cool for five minutes.

6 Crack the egg into a small bowl and beat.

7 Add the egg and vanilla to the cocoa mixture. Mix well.

8 Add the cocoa mixture to the dry ingredients. Beat with a wooden spoon until ingredients are blended well and smooth.

9 Fill each muffin cup about three-fourths full with the batter.

10 Place muffin tin in oven and bake for 20 minutes, or until a toothpick inserted near the center comes out clean.

11 Cool the muffins completely on a wire rack.

EYEBALL FROSTING

INGREDIENTS

3 tablespoons softened butter
3 ounces softened cream cheese
1 $\frac{2}{3}$ cups powdered sugar
$\frac{1}{2}$ teaspoon vanilla extract
red food coloring
green food coloring
12 chocolate chips

EQUIPMENT

medium mixing bowl
fork
wooden spoon
two small bowls
butter knife or spatula
two small plastic sandwich bags
kitchen scissors

STEPS

1. In the bowl, use a fork to mix the butter and cream cheese together until light and fluffy.

2. Add the powdered sugar and vanilla to the bowl. Then mix together with a wooden spoon until smooth.

3. Put about two tablespoons of white frosting into each of the small bowls. Mix a few drops of red food coloring into one small bowl to make red frosting. Use green food coloring in the other bowl.

4. Use a butter knife or spatula to top the cupcakes with the rest of the white frosting.

5. Spoon the red frosting into a small plastic sandwich bag. Squeeze the frosting into one corner. With scissors, snip the tip off of the corner to make a very small hole.

6. Gently squeeze the bag to decorate the cupcakes with blood-shot eyeball veins.

7. Spoon the green frosting into another plastic sandwich bag. Make a slightly bigger hole in the corner of the bag. Squeeze circles of green frosting onto the centers of the cupcakes.

8. Add a chocolate chip, point down, to the center of each green circle.

BLOODY BANDAGES

MAKES 24 TO 36 BANDAGES

Need a sweet but disgusting treat for your next Halloween party? Gross out your friends with these used bandages! Mmmmm, that glob of blood makes these crispy snacks taste so good.

BANDAGES

INGREDIENTS

1 cup whole wheat flour
1 cup all purpose flour
  (plus extra for kneading)
1/4 cup sugar
1/4 teaspoon salt
1 teaspoon cinnamon
1 teaspoon baking powder
1 large egg
1/4 cup vegetable oil
1/4 cup honey
2 tablespoons milk

EQUIPMENT

large mixing bowl
medium mixing bowl
plastic wrap
cooking spray
2 baking sheets
cutting board
rolling pin
sharp cooking knife
fork
wire rack

STEPS

1 Mix together the flours, sugar, salt, cinnamon, and baking powder in a large bowl.

2 Beat the egg in a medium bowl. Then mix in the oil, honey, and milk.

3 Add the wet mixture to the dry mixture and blend to make a stiff dough.

4 Wrap the dough in plastic wrap and chill in the refrigerator for at least 1 hour.

5 Preheat the oven to 375° F. Spray two baking sheets with cooking spray.

6 Take out the dough and knead it a few times on a well-floured cutting board. Then sprinkle flour on top of the dough and roll it out to 1/16-inch (0.12-cm) thick.

7 Cut the dough into 1- by 3-inch (2.5- by 7.6-cm) rectangles. Prick each rectangle a few times with a fork. Move the rectangles to the baking sheets.

8 Bake for 15 to 20 minutes or until golden.

9 Remove from oven and cool the bandages on the wire rack.

Try This!

To make quick and easy used bandages, you can use pre-made graham crackers. Just break them apart along the dotted lines before applying the frosting and jam.

GAUZE AND BLOOD

INGREDIENTS

3 tablespoons softened butter
3 ounces softened cream cheese
1 2/3 cups powdered sugar
1/2 teaspoon vanilla extract
strawberry jam

EQUIPMENT

small bowl
fork
wooden spoon
plastic sandwich bag
kitchen scissors

STEPS

1. In a small bowl, use a fork to mix the butter and cream cheese together until light and fluffy.

2. Add the powdered sugar and vanilla to the bowl and mix everything with a wooden spoon until smooth.

3. Spoon some of the frosting into the plastic sandwich bag. Squeeze it into one of the lower corners. Snip the tip off the corner with scissors. Squeeze the white frosting onto the center of each bandage in a square shape.

4. Add a glob of strawberry jam to the center to simulate blood.

READ MORE

Cook, Deanna F. *Cooking Class: 57 Fun Recipes Kids Will Love to Make (and Eat!)* North Adams, Mass.: Storey Publishing, 2015.

Jorgensen, Katrina. *Football Party Recipes: Delicious Ideas for the Big Event.* Football Cookbooks. North Mankato, Minn.: Capstone Press, 2015.

Tjernagel, Kelsi Turner. *Gross Recipes.* Gross Guides. North Mankato, Minn.: Capstone Press, 2013.

INTERNET SITES

FactHound offers a safe, fun way to find Internet sites related to this book. All of the sites on Facthound have been researched by our staff.

Here's all you do:
Visit *www.facthound.com*
Type in this code: 9781515738121

Super-cool stuff! Check out projects, games and lots more at **www.capstonekids.com**